UNIVERSITY OF **ILLINOIS** PRESS

REVIEW COPY

Between the Museum and the City
Douglas Garofalo, Foreword by Robert
Fitzpatrick and Judith Kirshner, Introduction by
Elizabeth A.T. Smith

U.S. Cloth Price: $25
Publication Date: March 15, 2004

Contact: Danielle Wilberg (217) 244-4689

Please send TWO copies of your review to:

University of Illinois Press
1325 South Oak Street
Champaign, IL 61820-6903
Fax: (217) 244-8082

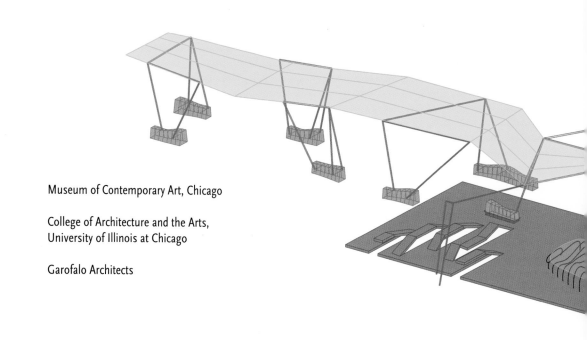

Museum of Contemporary Art, Chicago

College of Architecture and the Arts,
University of Illinois at Chicago

Garofalo Architects

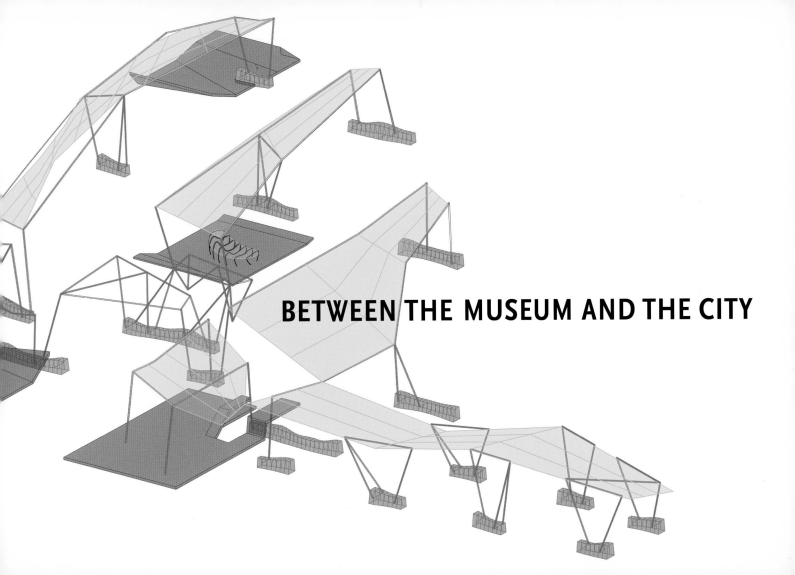

BETWEEN THE MUSEUM AND THE CITY

Garofalo Architects: Between the Museum and the City was on view at the Museum of Contemporary Art, Chicago (MCA), May 3 to October 14, 2003, and was co-organized by the MCA and the College of Architecture and the Arts, University of Illinois at Chicago (CAA/UIC).

Support for this project was generously provided by Nancy and Sanfred Koltun; the National Endowment for the Arts, a federal agency; and the Graham Foundation for Advanced Studies in the Fine Arts.

Additional support for programming on architecture is provided by The Richard H. Driehaus Foundation.

Support for this catalogue was generously provided by U.S. Equities Realty.

In-kind support was provided by the Chicago Park District, Crown Construction, Thornton Tomasetti Engineers, Dukane Precast, Anton Metal Works, Unistrut Corporation, iLight, Inc., and Garofalo Architects, Inc.

The MCA is a nonprofit, tax-exempt organization. The MCA's exhibitions, programming, and operations are member supported and privately funded through contributions from individuals, corporations, and foundations. Additional support is provided through the Illinois Arts Council, a state agency. Air transportation services are provided by American Airlines, the official airline of the Museum of Contemporary Art.

ISBN 0-933856-82-2   Library of Congress Catalog Number: 2003115370

Produced by the Publications Department of the Museum of Contemporary Art, Chicago. Edited by Kari Dahlgren, Associate Director of Publications. Designed by Hal Kugeler, Director of Design and Publications. Printing by Sheffield Press, Hammond, Ind. Binding by Zonne Bookbinders, Chicago

This book is distributed by University of Illinois Press, 1325 South Oak Street, Champaign, Ill. 61820-6903. 800.537.5487 www.press.uillinois.edu

Contents

Foreword

Overlaid across the plaza and staircase rising to the entrance of the Museum of Contemporary Art and spilling into Seneca Park across the street, *Between the Museum and the City* presented an unexpected experience for museum-goers and urban dwellers. An eccentric steel structure of linear supports anchored by curvy, concrete forms and highlighted by bright-yellow awnings, the installation functionally and visually flaunted its cheerful spontaneity in the face of the modernist demeanor of the museum. Its framework encouraged audiences to explore and experience the contemporary art within as new itineraries mapped and crisscrossed the grand space.

Between the Museum and the City has continued a history of the MCA and UIC working together, and it was enormously gratifying for our two institutions to collaborate on this project. With the MCA's James W. Alsdorf Chief Curator Elizabeth Smith; Greg Cameron, Associate Director and Chief Development Officer; and Zhivka Valiavicharska, Marjorie Susman Curatorial Fellow, architect Douglas Garofalo orchestrated a series of discussions for this project about the social function of architecture within the context of the local urban environment, including an unusual diversity of people of different ages and backgrounds in its design, execution, and documentation.

We are grateful to our many colleagues at the MCA and UIC for their creativity and leadership during the course of this project. At the MCA, we thank Karla Loring, Director of Media Relations; Hal Kugeler, Director of Design and Publications; Kari Dahlgren, Associate Director of Publications; Stephen Hokanson, Senior Preparator; and Michal Raz-Russo, Photographer. At UIC, we acknowledge Jane M. Saks, Director of Advancement for the College of Architecture and the Arts; Hannah Higgins, Associate Professor of Art History; and the students in UIC's spring 2003 seminar Public(s) Art(s). Megan McDonald, Lakefront Region Manager for the Chicago Park District, was enormously helpful.

Numerous individuals and organizations were enthusiastic in their support for this project. We are indebted to Nancy and Sanfred Koltun, the National Endowment for the Arts, and the Graham Foundation for Advanced Studies in the Fine Arts for their great generosity, and we are also grateful to Susan and Lewis Manilow, Judith Neisser, and the University of Illinois at Chicago Institute for the Humanities. We also thank The Richard H. Driehaus Foundation for their support of programming on architecture at the MCA. We are sincerely grateful to U.S. Equities Realty and its chairman, Robert A. Wislow, for underwriting this publication, thereby allowing us to create a permanent record for an ephemeral project. We also thank Sharon Burge, Vice President of Marketing at U.S. Equities Realty, for her assistance with this publication.

Lastly, we thank Douglas Garofalo and his dedicated staff, especially project manager Julie Flohr, for their vision and commitment to this truly collaborative project.

Robert Fitzpatrick
Pritzker Director
Museum of Contemporary Art, Chicago

Judith Russi Kirshner
Dean
College of Architecture and the Arts,
University of Illinois at Chicago

Introduction
Elizabeth A.T. Smith

James W. Alsdorf Chief Curator
Museum of Contemporary Art, Chicago

Garofalo Architects' project *Between the Museum and the City* resulted from an unprecedented collaboration between the Museum of Contemporary Art and the College of Architecture and the Arts, University of Illinois at Chicago. Its foremost goal was to stimulate the creation of new architectural work as an extension of the MCA's programmatic mandate to engage with and foster the creative processes of living artists. Another significant goal was to provide an interactive zone between the museum building and the city itself, offering urban amenities for visitors and residents, extending the museum's visibility, and educating new audiences. Collaborating with the UIC College of Architecture and the Arts, where architect Douglas Garofalo is a faculty member, enabled the MCA to articulate and develop these goals in tandem with an analytical and educational process led by the College. The resulting project was both architecturally and programmatically innovative, with theory and practice merging, intersecting, and informing one another.

The unique character of this project took shape not only from the investigatory, creative approach undertaken by Garofalo Architects to the design problem itself, but also from the generative role that academic and cultural institutions can play in the public sphere when engaging directly with design related to city forms and function. Following Garofalo's acceptance of the MCA's invitation to develop what was envisioned as the first in a series of temporary architectural projects to animate its front plaza, a joint MCA-UIC project team undertook a series of discussions during the course of several months to define the parameters and goals of the collaboration. These ranged from small, in-house working sessions to larger public forums to which members of the community and civic leaders were invited to observe and comment. Thus a wide spectrum of people participated in the dialogue, considering an expansive range of issues. Simultaneously, UIC's curriculum on public space issues as well as construction and fabrication techniques related to temporary structures formed a crucial part of the project's development and influenced its final form.

Beginning work on their concepts for the project in late fall 2002, Garofalo Architects realized the final structure less than six months later. The intensive initial phase of analysis, theorizing, and design development at the museum, in the architects' studio, and in the classroom was followed by experimentation with materials, off-site fabrication of key elements, and the beginnings of assembly of the structure itself in the public space of the museum's plaza by April 2003. An experimental sensibility

predominated throughout, both with regard to innovation with form and materials, and concerning possibilities surrounding the generative role of the structure in the social sphere of public space. Careful attention to the exigencies of a modest budget and a condensed time frame were also characteristic. During its six months of residency in the plaza, the structure served as a stage set for performances and a gathering place for educational programs related to architecture; it enveloped a weekly farmers market; its series of zoned and shaded spaces provided a setting for MCA staff meetings, lunchtime gatherings, and even nighttime dinner parties; its curvaceous yellow seating units offered a respite for bicycle messengers, museum visitors, and tourists who often posed for photographs there.

Between the Museum and the City accomplished the bridging of a cultural and educational institution with the public realm both literally and symbolically. This partnership between two major Chicago institutions and a significant emerging talent in the field of architecture not only reinforced an ongoing history of collaboration and commitment to meaningful audience development between the MCA and UIC but helped bring attention to innovative architectural practice in Chicago as a creative contribution of visual significance in our city.

The temporary structure was intended to feature innovative contemporary architectural thought while extending the MCA's activities into an interactive public space.

— Elizabeth A. T. Smith

Between the Museum and the City Douglas Garofalo

What could public space mean in the context of a contemporary art museum? How is this question skewed by the temporary nature of installations? In the particular case of the Museum of Contemporary Art in Chicago these questions are further framed by the building itself, designed by Josef Paul Kleihues and completed in 1996. From its stark front plaza, to its monumental staircase that elevates the institution above the street, to its right-angled geometry, this is a building that projects ideas of hierarchy and monumentality that are incongruous with contemporary sensibilities. Most importantly, the structure intimidates already-suspicious passersby from gathering outside or coming in to contemplate contemporary works of art.[1]

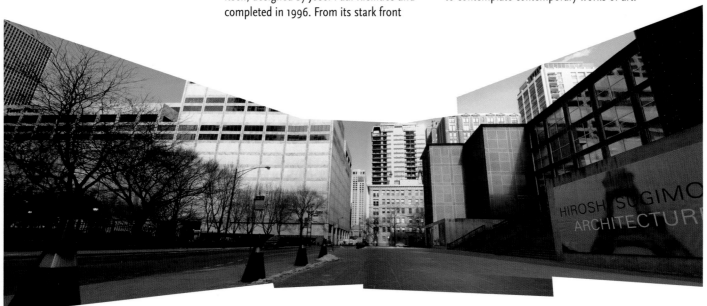

In the latter part of 2002 my firm was asked to be the first to participate in a new program at the MCA, a series of annual commissions for architects and artists to design and construct works for the front plaza. Occupying the public space for six months, our temporary project would house a series of events extending the institution's programmatic, educational, and outreach functions, and stimulating the genesis of new public uses for the plaza.[2]

The temporary nature of the project and its limited budget encouraged architectural experimentation. Our task as architects was to address the MCA's goal by linking the museum building with its surroundings. We came to understand this linking as a sort of weaving. The result was a series of abstract systems that intermingled on the stairs and across the plaza, offering a variety of possible seating and reclining options in sun and shade, a cafe counter, and flexible spaces for performances, gatherings, and the weekly farmers market. All this on a site deemed "placeless" by many.

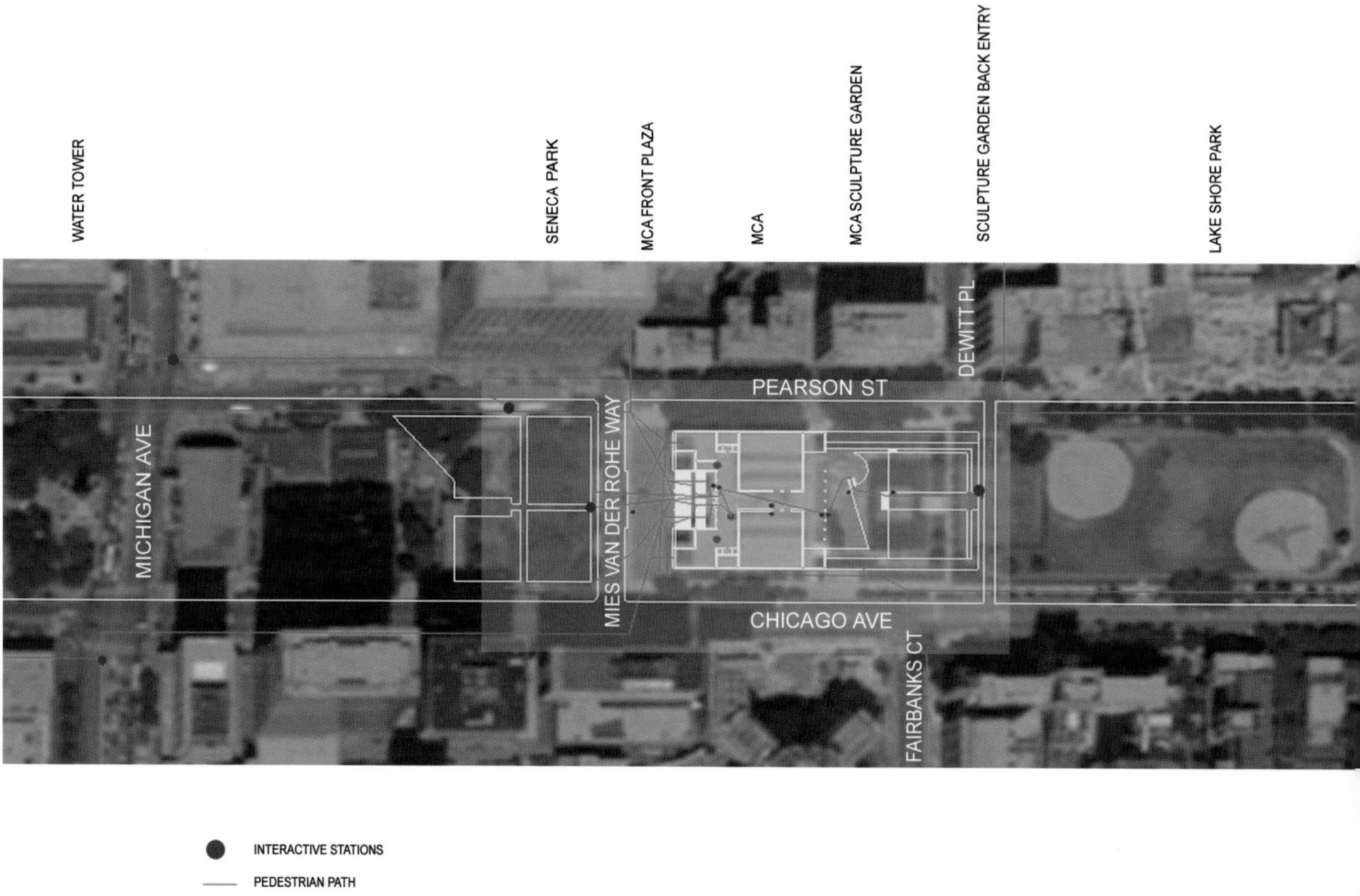

WATER TOWER

SENECA PARK

MCA FRONT PLAZA

MCA

MCA SCULPTURE GARDEN

SCULPTURE GARDEN BACK ENTRY

LAKE SHORE PARK

DEWITT PL

PEARSON ST

MICHIGAN AVE

MIES VAN DER ROHE WAY

CHICAGO AVE

FAIRBANKS CT

● INTERACTIVE STATIONS

— PEDESTRIAN PATH

LAKEFRONT BICYCLE PATH

LAKE MICHIGAN

LAKE SHORE DRIVE

Site Analysis

Our sense of the term *site* refers to the debate about public space: Can the public realm be more than shopping? Need it be sanitized, surveyed, and domesticated to the point of being invisible for it to be comfortable? Must public space have a certain meaning or specific identity that the public always comprehends? Our project was meant to be open, in a real sense incomplete without the presence of bodies *and* minds: we do not believe experimental, thought-provoking work is incompatible with function and comfort, and nowhere are these conceits more appropriate than in a public space in front of a contemporary art museum. Beyond the basic function of reinventing the connection of the MCA to the street, we attempted to produce a challenging and engaging system of spaces that would act less like a piece of sculpture and more like a landscape, a set of networked structures that would extend from the MCA to capture interest and hold activity.

The MCA's seeming disjunction with its surroundings — busy commercial and recreational attractions such as Michigan Avenue and Lake Michigan — informed our early conceptual thinking. In discussions with MCA staff, we mapped the pedestrian traffic around and within the museum to understand the continuity between interior and exterior. These mappings led to ideas of an abstract structure that could respond to local pedestrian traffic and to programmed activities by gathering and relating the museum's plaza, lobby, and sculpture garden with Seneca Park, Michigan Avenue, and even Lake Michigan.

15

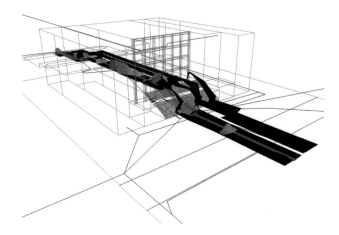

Site Analysis

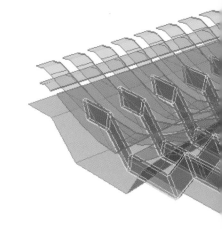

Strategies

The concept of weaving emerged from the complexity of the site, the variety of possible and potential uses for the plaza, and in discussions with MCA staff. At the urban scale, weaving suggests stitching the detached institution into the fabric of the city. As an architectural technique it allows high degrees of local difference (in pattern, color, material, program, form, etc.) that are nevertheless visible as part of a larger composition. Weaving is also based on hierarchy and geometry, much as the building is based on the Chicago grid. But weaving can also imply a tactility and detail at the scale of a body. Many of our choices for configuration, geometry, material, and color were therefore based not on a singular formal vision, but on the idea of variably textured, interlaced sets of spaces within spaces that suggest continuity with the museum's contents and the city. The makeup of this weave consisted of steel flyovers, fabric clouds, concrete ribbons, wooden oases, soft islands, and a lighting swarm.

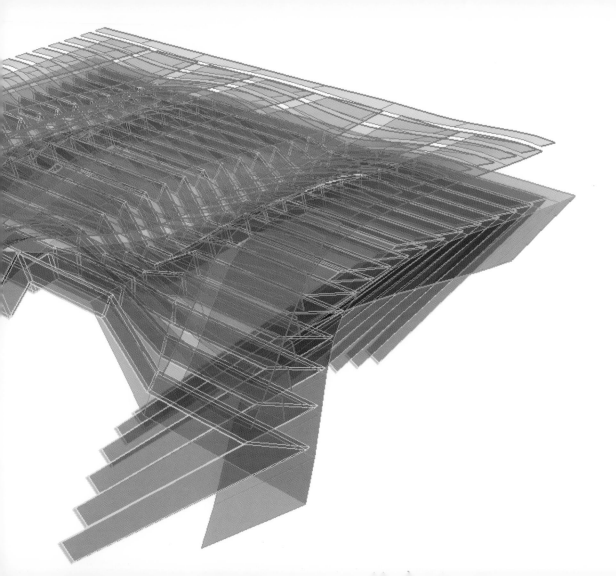

Strategies

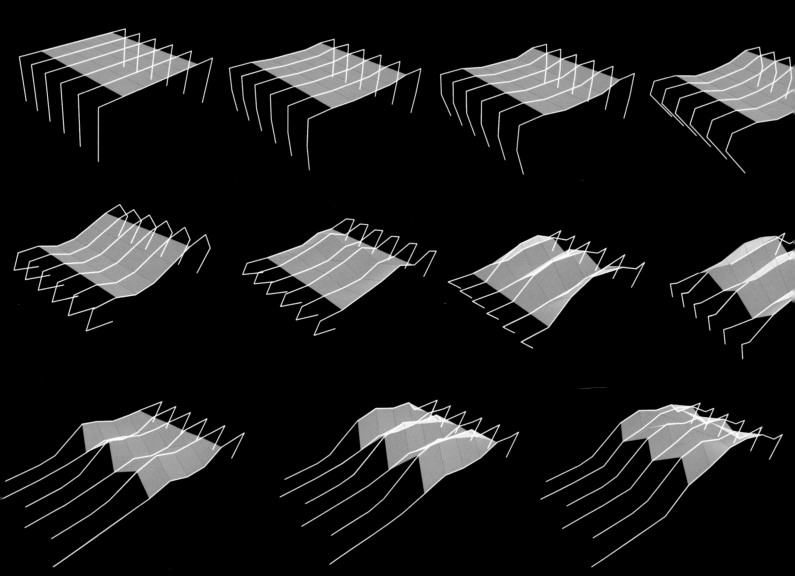

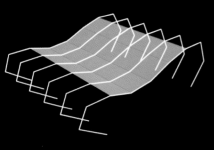

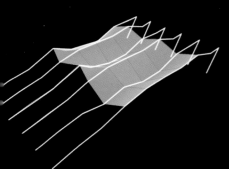

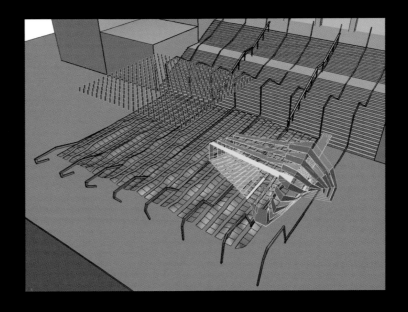

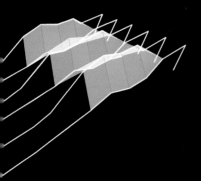

Strategies

Early sketches and conceptual models were presented at the first schematic meeting at Garofalo Architects' offices in January, 2003. Early stick-figure models incorporated pipe cleaners, twist-ties, and paper clips.

Strategies

The deterritorializatio
produced liberating e
strictures of place-bo
fluidity of a migrator
possibilities for the p
identities, allegiances

f the site has
cts, displacing the
d identities with the
nodel, introducing
duction of multiple
nd meanings.

— Miwon Kwon [3]

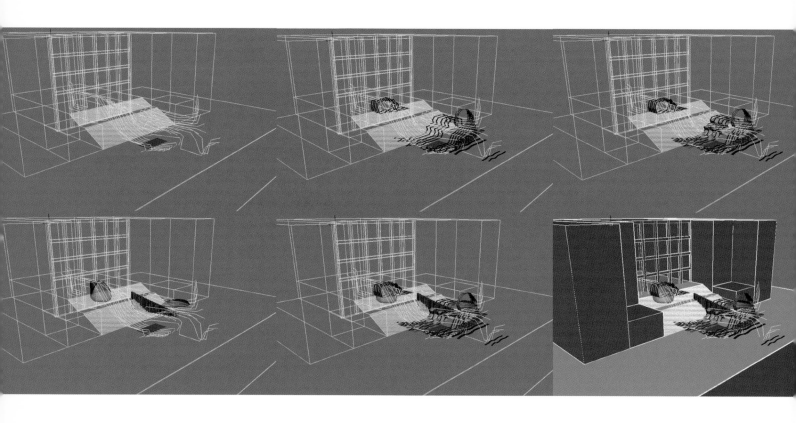

Between the Museum and the City

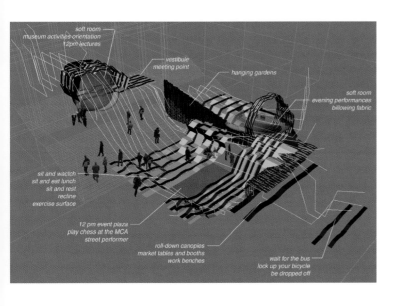

soft room
museum activities orientation
12pm lectures

vestibule
meeting point

hanging gardens

soft room
evening performances
billowing fabric

sit and wactch
sit and eat lunch
sit and rest
recline
exercise surface

12 pm event plaza
play chess at the MCA
street performer

roll-down canopies
market tables and booths
work benches

wait for the bus
lock up your bicycle
be dropped off

One particular interest of ours became the problem of scale in the existing plaza. How could we introduce texture, material, and surface in a way that would make the space more tactile? Weaving seemed to be a possible solution.

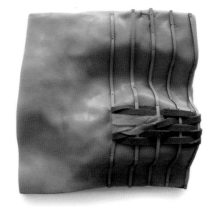

Strategies

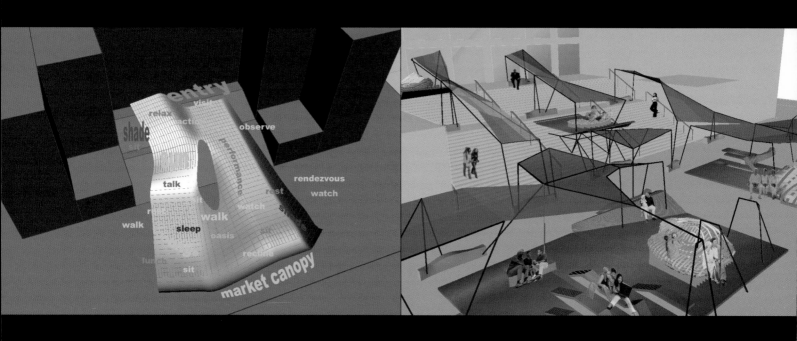

Between the Museum and the City

STEEL FLYOVERS

Steel struts, or flyovers, offered support for the overhead shade canopies and served as channels for electrical wires. They were initially conceived as a giant animated "stick figure" that would move through the building and plaza. This stick figure was meant to have multiple meanings. As a structure it was merely a sketch of a possible architecture; it had the scale and proportions of the gridded facade, and therefore seemed to tumble and crawl across the stairs and the plaza; it was conceived to be extendable. It suggested a scaffold for interpretation,

activity, and performance. More parts could be added to the system, as happened late in the project's life.[4] The resulting dynamic structure fully spread onto the stairs and the plaza, echoing the strong geometric forms of the MCA building yet offering the idea that strong geometry can also exhibit qualities of humility: the structure suggested a kneeling organism with legs dutifully arranged to invite inhabitation, an antithesis to the rigid grids of typical downtown architecture. This idea of tolerance extended to the fabrication of the structure as well, as this system allowed for many adjustments on site without compromise to the overall effect. We developed a custom joint designed to give three-dimensional flexibility to the structure, for use with an off-the-shelf system of steel channels, both of which enabled us to keep designing on site as we built. These joints have numerous pull points to accept vinyl-coated steel cables, putting the entire system in tension to resist wind loads.

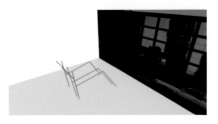

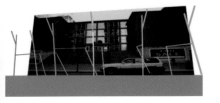

Steel Flyovers

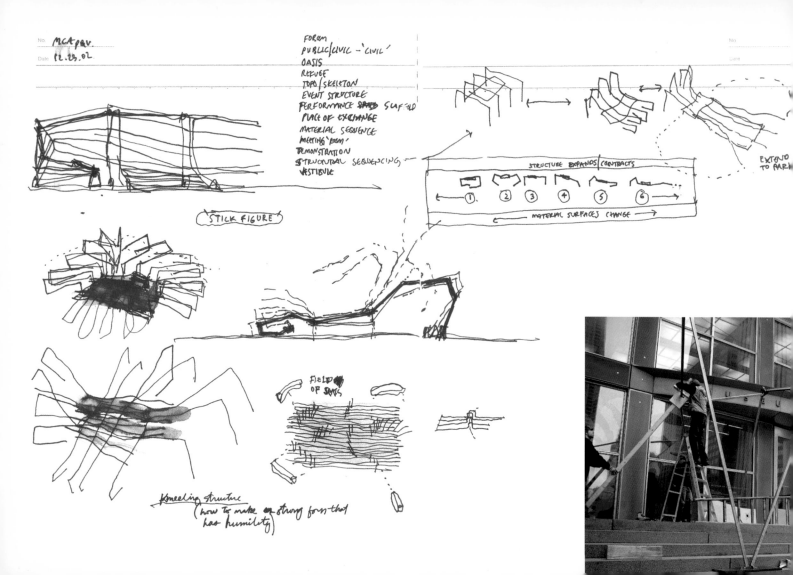

No. MCA pav.
Date 12.23.02

FORUM
PUBLIC/CIVIC - 'CIVIL'
OASIS
REFUGE
TOPO / SKELETON
EVENT STRUCTURE
PERFORMANCE STAGE SCAFFOLD
PLACE OF EXCHANGE
MATERIAL SEQUENCE
MEETING 'ROOM'
DEMONSTRATION
STRUCTURAL SEQUENCING
VESTIBULE

EXTEND TO PARK

STRUCTURE EXPANDS/CONTRACTS

① ② ③ ④ ⑤ ⑥

MATERIAL SURFACES CHANGE

STICK FIGURE

FIELD OF STIKS

kneeling structure
(how to make a strong form that
has humility)

The stick figure idea remained throughout the project, offering perhaps the most salient counterpoint to the geometry of the building. At one point during the UIC seminar on public space, a student suggested the possibility for the system to travel to other institutions, where it could perform similar functions as a traveling public space system.

Steel Flyovers

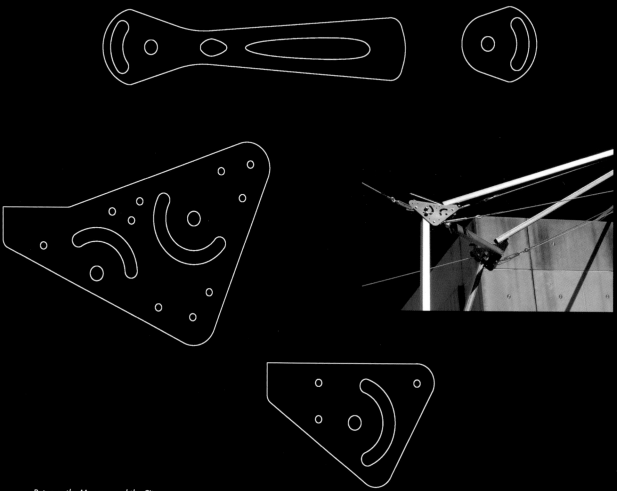

36

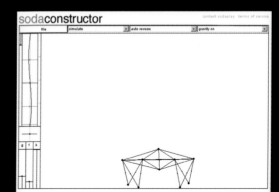

38

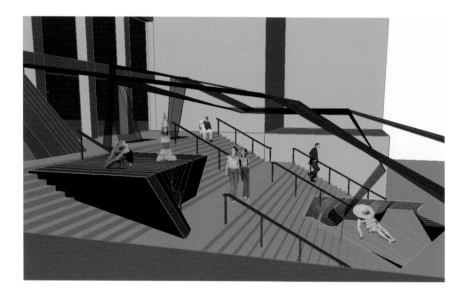

The steel flyovers were
meant both to animate
the plaza and to support
canopies that would
provide color and shade.

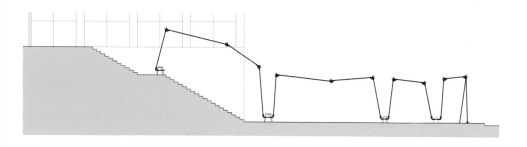
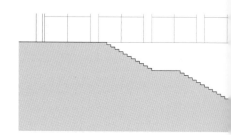

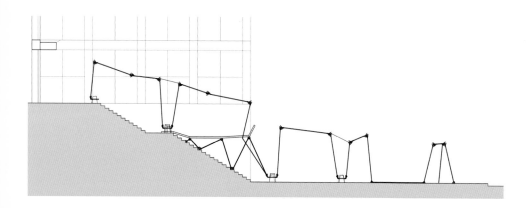
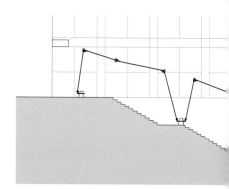

Between the Museum and the City

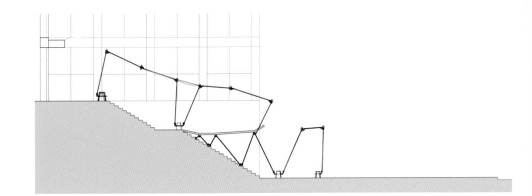

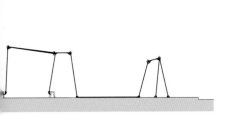

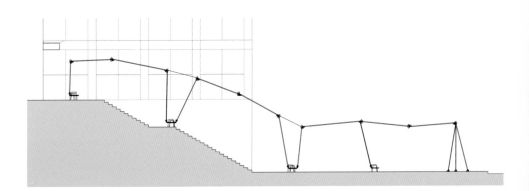

Steel Flyovers

FABRIC CLOUDS

Attached to the steel flyovers, fabric canopies initially thought of as "clouds" provided shade on the plaza, which can be extremely hot in mid-summer. The canopies, conceived as an aesthetic as well as a functional element, visually connected the architectural elements as a whole and brought color to the gray environment. Our initial scheme included two mobile, winglike fabric canopies that would expand and contract in order to house the weekly farmers market. Consultation with engineers[5] and experiments with various materials showed that any large surface of fabric stretched onto the steel structure would not withstand strong winds. This led to the final design of smaller identical fabric panels arranged in a dynamic pattern. The metaphor of the cloud gave way to a repetitive system of units that built up to form the canopies, much as the leaves of trees combine into one swaying mass of green, as in Seneca Park across the street.

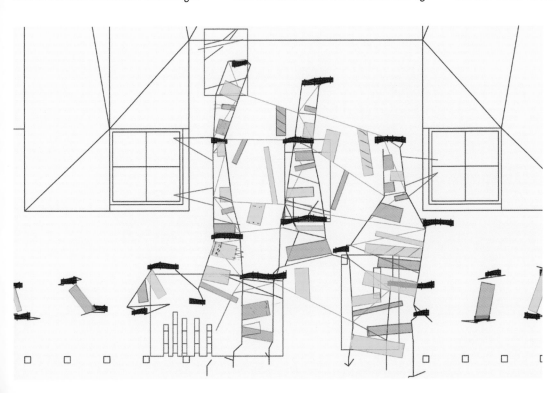

Fabric Clouds

Between the Museum and the City

Fabric Clouds

Architecture — its social relevance and formal invention — cannot be dissociated from the events that "happen" in it.

— Bernard Tschumi

Between the Museum and the City

We looked at parachutes and canopies of all kinds. Students from UIC went so far as to fly kites on site in February to get a sense of the wind patterns. We were surprised at how open the fabric had to be to avoid the wind uplift stressing the steel system beyond capacity.

Fabric Clouds

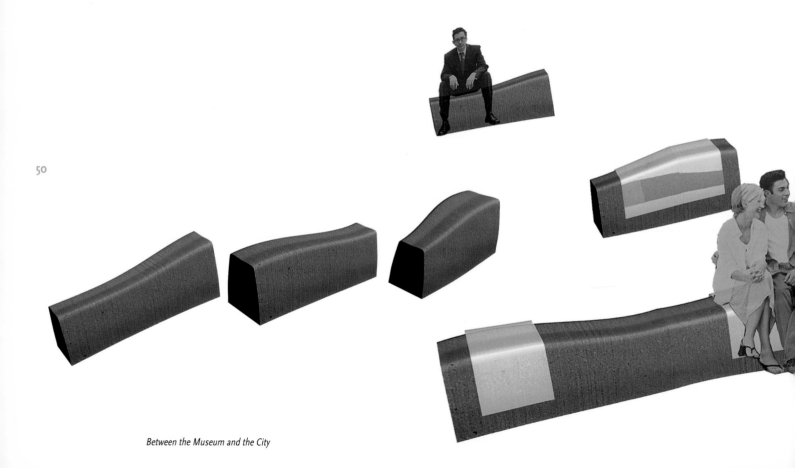

Between the Museum and the City

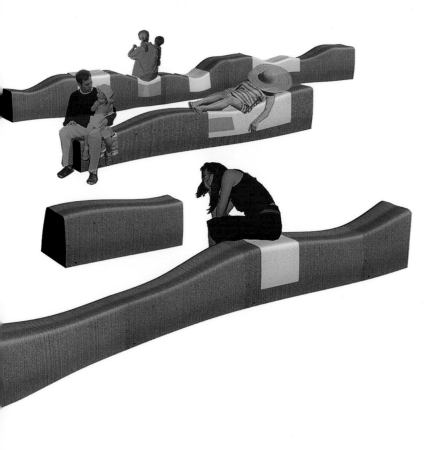

CONCRETE RIBBONS

The temporary nature of this project dictated certain limitations, which determined to a great extent the design and materials used in the installation, particularly how the entire structure would be anchored safely to the plaza and steps. The biggest challenge was the museum's requirement not to attach anything to the building or plaza. In response, we designed a ribbonlike set of supports for the steel structure. In terms of the overall weave these elements would cut across the grain of the stick figure scampering overhead and the directional wooden oases below. Unlike the segmented and skeletal structure, however, these elements were envisioned as sinewy, wavelike shapes with matching ends such that their placement could redirect the existing pedestrian traffic patterns and offer places to sit and recline. We developed three shapes that were produced in steel molds; concrete casting began a month prior to installation at the rate of three a day.[6] Each of the concrete casts weighs approximately 2,300 pounds, offsetting the intense winds that pressurize the canopies overhead.

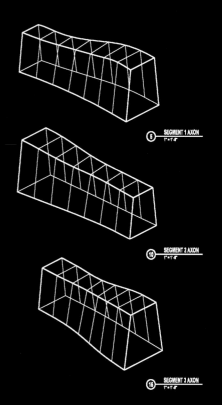

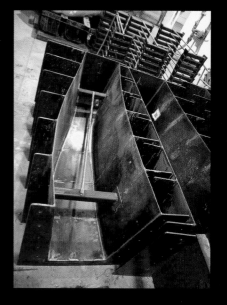

SEGMENT 1 AXON
1" = 1'-0"

SEGMENT 2 AXON
1" = 1'-0"

SEGMENT 3 AXON
1" = 1'-0"

Between the Museum and the City

Concrete Ribbons

Almost immediately upon setting the concrete ribbons in place we observed how the public interpreted them. The skateboarders came first, testing the curves on the underside of their boards, and when the sun came out, sunbathers appeared seemingly out of nowhere.

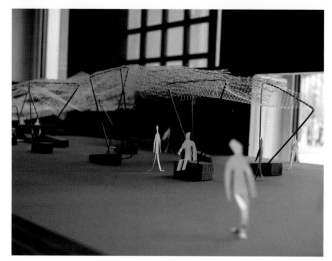

WOODEN OASES

The wooden platforms derived directly from a desire to occupy the plaza with numerous smaller spaces to break down the monumental scale of the plaza. These decks offered important spatial definition and lighter color, but also a warmer material that absorbed more sound than the surrounding granite and concrete. These oases, like the concrete ribbons, were intended to direct pedestrian traffic and allow benches and counters to undulate and unfold to various heights. One of these was elevated midway up the stairs as a possible place for performances and speeches, though it existed also as a simple balcony from which to survey the plaza, hold a meeting, or take a nap in relative privacy from the sidewalk below.

Wooden Oases

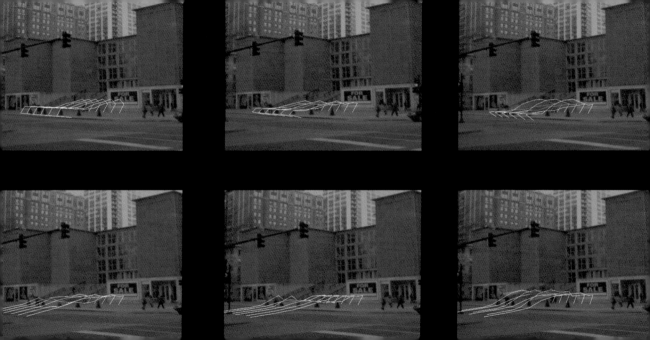

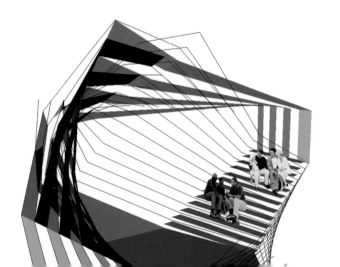

Repetition has always been a part of construction and fabrication processes. We wanted to explore with this project how variation would animate various spaces and functions, how sequences of material could suggest movement and enclosure.

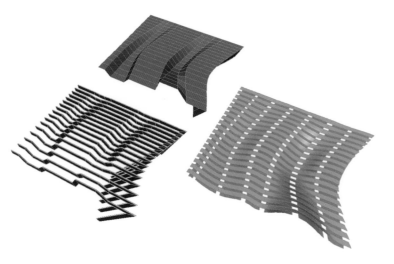

Wooden Oases

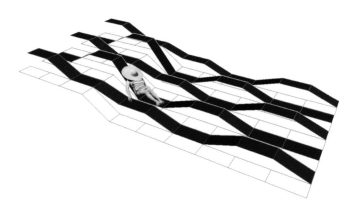

Between the Museum and the City

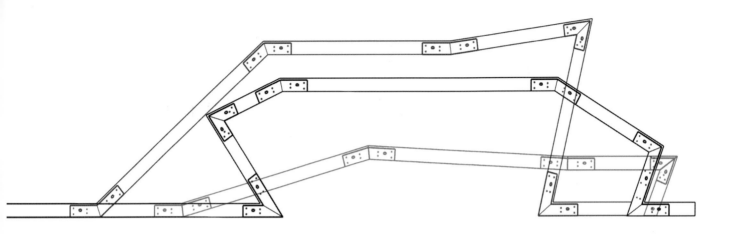

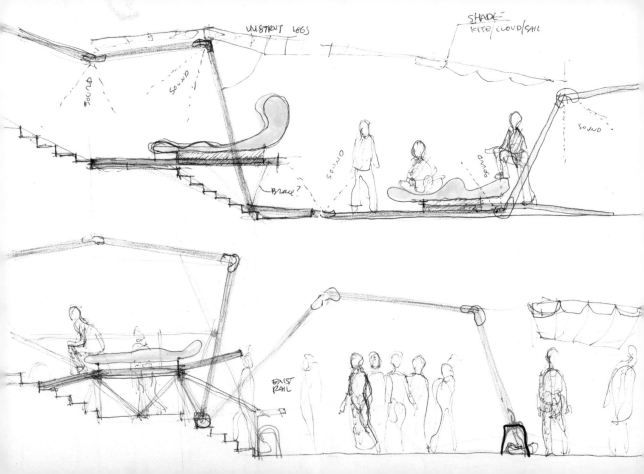

UNISTRUT LEGS

SHADE
KITE/CLOUD/SAIL

SOUND

SOUND

SOUND

SOUND

SOUND

SOUND

Brace?

EXIST RAIL

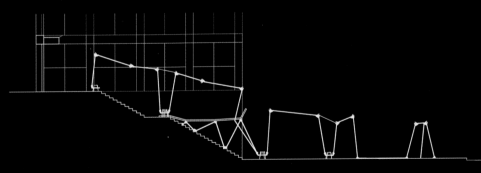

All the wood elements were built with the members running east-west. This was to create a weave with the concrete ribbons, which were oriented north-south. Perhaps more importantly, the linearity of the wood connects the museum to the street.

Wooden Oases

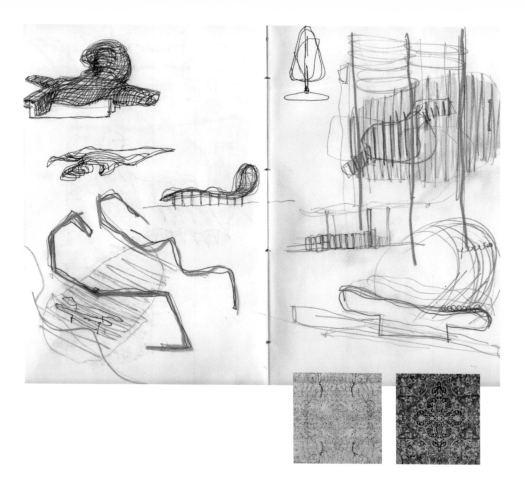

68

SOFT ISLANDS

The islands were conceived as the center points of activity, and served as the visual and physical focus of the installation—their bright color, detailed surface, and inviting shape brought softness to the space and enticed visitors to touch, sit on, and lounge in them. Indeed these seemed to be the most popular elements. At times the public lined up to try these elements, and we witnessed couples arriving at night by car to run up to the most remote island on the elevated deck to engage in ten minutes of private activity. The initial idea for the forms resembled large semitransparent rooms with soft flexible walls, and we had considered a more traditional, partially enclosed performance area. Smaller zones developed after the architects and museum staff discussed functional and safety issues for the plaza; we agreed that more interesting potential could be derived from nontraditional elements, with artists reacting to the unconventional nature of the spaces and forms. The techniques used to "weave" the bright yellow islands echo those used in traditional crafts like basket weaving. However, the industrial materials—gas pipe, cellular foam, twist-ties, wire-coated cable, and bungee cord—strikingly contrast the natural materials commonly used in traditional weavings.[7]

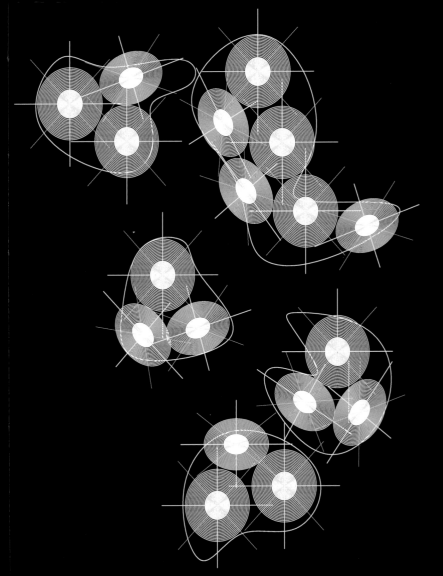

Soft Islands

The MCA's commitment to temp
inspired way to promote learnin
computer simulation but from rea
team's
to scar
of the

ry, yearly installations is an
bout what works, not from a
vorld experience. The Garofalo
ght, insectlike structures stand
er across the impassive surfaces
A in small, happy rebellion.

— Lynn Becker, *Chicago Reader*

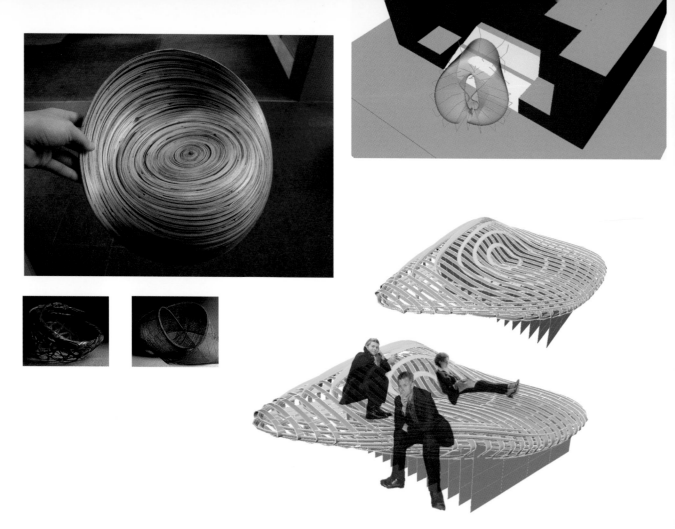

74

Between the Museum and the City

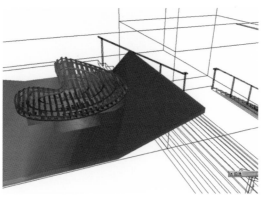

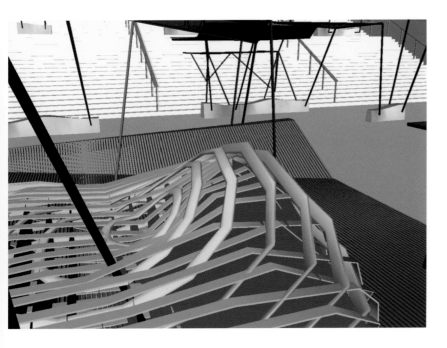

When designing the project, we went to an extremely interesting exhibition on Japanese basket weaving, which had traditional and contemporary pieces. The techniques and methods were inspiring and humbling — the intricacy and sophistication rivaled anything we could produce using computers.

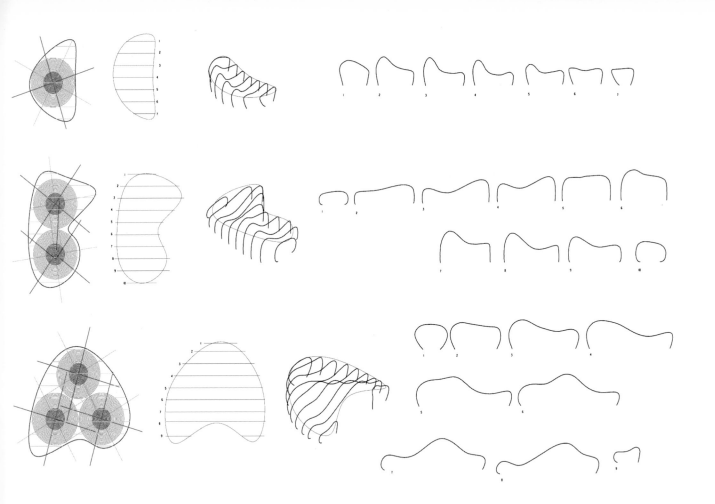

Soft Islands

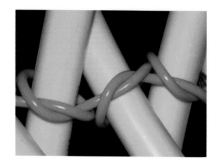

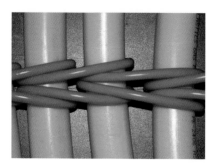

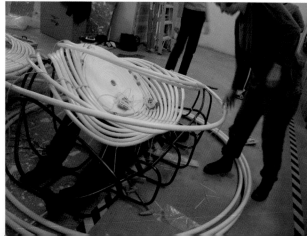

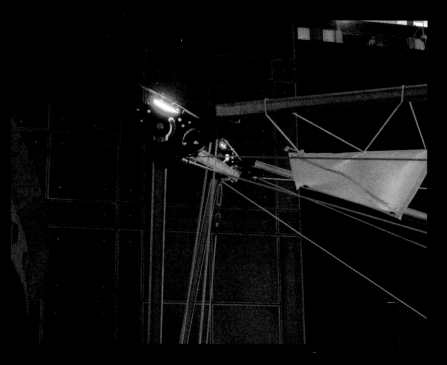

LIGHTING SWARM

To activate the space at night, we incorporated artificial lights in various elements of the project. Four-inch LED light strips were suspended within each steel joint, highlighting the articulation of the steel channels. Larger strips were randomly embedded within the surfaces of the wooden decks. The tape sewn onto the fabric panels reflected light during the day and the night. The effect of the repetitive and dispersed light sources resembled a swarm of fireflies in the summertime.

80

Epilogue

Our attempt was to put in place a distinctive, experimental structure to draw interest to and use of the museum by animating the plaza and steps. As a weave it was meant to introduce a variety of materials with a direct connection to the body through repetition and texture, without sacrificing the need to structure the space as a place of urban gathering. This structure was not quite architecture and not sculpture, neither literally landscape nor conventional plaza design, yet it demonstrated all of these notions for the purposes of eliciting various interpretations and activities, by the public, by artists, curators, performers, educators, and anyone else interested in getting more out of civic space than what is typically expected from the public realm. Of course we all have differing desires and definitions of this realm. It is contested at best, though it is hard to understand the debate about public space unless one happens to be directly involved with it, as was the case in recent anti-war

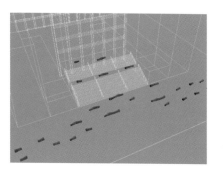 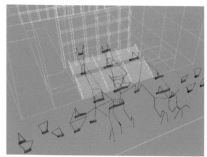 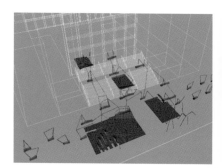

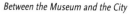

Between the Museum and the City

demonstrations across the country, and particularly those in Chicago that took place in early 2003.

Not everyone understood what we tried to accomplish with this commission. Some came away confused at what it was supposed to represent, unsure how it was meant to function, unable or unwilling to think beyond conventional notions of a plaza. Others didn't ask, preferring instead to act, to participate, to put the plaza and structure to use and to describe it for themselves and to others, and maybe to go into the museum. Optimistically, we as architects would like to believe we can and should accommodate all; at the same time, we know that consensus and experimentation have deep incompatibilities. Perhaps these oppositions must always be related and sustained if we are to have successful public works of architecture.

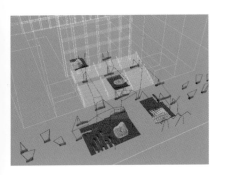 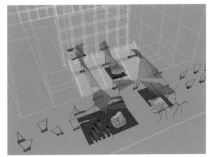 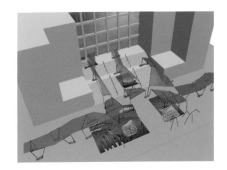

1 The MCA has presented admirable programs on the plaza in the past, with various performances and temporary sculptures. At moments the architectural and urban constraints of the building have been overcome or pushed to background as in Redmoon Theater's performance *Galway's Shadow* in 2001, when the facade was turned into a giant surface for shadow puppetry (see p. 92).

2 The installation, entitled *Garofalo Architects: Between the Museum and the City,* was curated by Elizabeth Smith, the James W. Alsdorf Chief Curator at the MCA, in collaboration with Judith Russi Kirshner, Dean of the College of Architecture and the Arts at the UIC.

3 Miwon Kwon sees opportunity in our globalized, digitized, and increasingly homogeneous world. She makes a compelling argument for what she terms "relational specificity," a practice that holds and maintains the tensions of difference for the purposes of making place. "This means addressing the uneven conditions of adjacencies and distances *between* one thing, one person, one place, one thought, one fragment *next* to another, rather than invoking equivalencies via one thing *after* another." From *One Place After Another: Site Specific Art and Locational Identity* (Cambridge, Mass.: MIT Press, 2002).

4 An additional piece was installed in Seneca Park across the street from the MCA to further the intended ideas of civic connection.

5 As we do with most of our work, we collaborated on this project with Joseph Burns of Thornton Tomasetti Engineers for all structural analysis.

6 Dukane Precast generously cast each piece from the steel molds we provided; Anton Metal Works fabricated these molds and much of the other steel work.

7 Graduate students in an architecture elective class at the University of Illinois at Chicago, School of Architecture assisted with the design, prototype, and execution of the islands, as well as on-site construction.

Components from *Between the Museum and the City* travelled to the Carnegie Museum in Pittsburgh to be reconfigured as an animated public space system. The exhibition, curated by Ray Ryan, situated components inside and outside the museum.

84

Between the Museum and the City

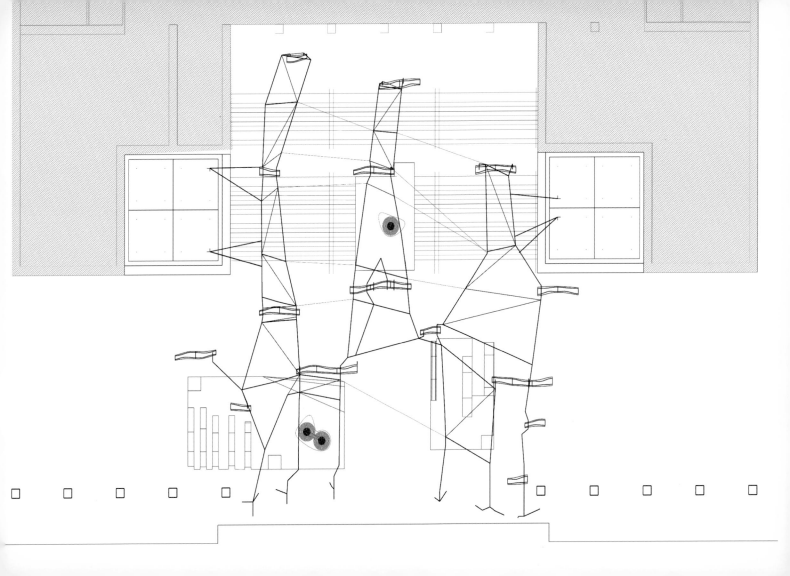

Between Art and Architecture Judith Russi Kirshner

Dean, College of Architecture and the Arts, University of Illinois at Chicago

Garofalo Architects' *Between the Museum and the City* straddled a history of temporary buildings and celebratory pavilions in Chicago and beyond; as intervention it referred to the power of "place" at the same time that it realized the connection between high culture and civic play. A freewheeling place-maker, like agitprop, it served its informational purpose well, attracting consumers from Michigan Avenue to the Museum of Contemporary Art's galleries. And just as the concept of space can be expressed in social, economic, and political vocabularies, so too can its use be symbolic and paradoxical.

The concept of an ideal urban space that is both public property and private place has been frequently theorized, but for this project, Garofalo Architects' user-friendly interface provided the chance to experience an experimental topography spread-eagled on the MCA plaza. Architect and critic Bernard Tschumi's notion that "architecture — its social relevance and

Between the Museum and the City

formal invention — cannot be dissociated from the events that 'happen' in it"[1] could be assumed as the departure point for Garofalo's project. Here, too, the invitation to participate augmented the debates that surround the politics, meaning, and functions of public space. Visitors found that the plaza now offered spaces for relaxation, even spontaneous pleasure, with platforms of wooden slats set like little stages and large nests woven of yellow cords. Seizing the potential for theater, such a space, according to Tschumi, "ceases to be a backdrop for actions, becoming the action itself."[2] This notion reinforces the link between Garofalo Architects' computer animations and the schematic layout that was generated. In accordance with the collaborative curatorial vision, the designers treated the facade as surface whose strict geometric grid and transparency allowed one to see through the building east to the lake. Metaphorically, the grid could be relaxed and portrayed as a stick figure striding across the front plaza, so that the project appeared to be a witty, animated version of the grid underlying the museum's geometry. By the same token, spectators in this kind of scheme become actors in an urban per-

formance. *Between the Museum and the City* was purposefully provocative; it revealed the formal and ideological contradictions between the host structure and the rambling narrative of the plaza design.

A crossover between architectural requirements and artistic imagination, Garofalo Architects' project explored the intersections of spatial and temporal coordinates, architecture and collective performance. *Between the Museum and the City* delivered a timely rather than timeless use of urban space, a quality underscored by the computer-generated graphics that provided the conceptual animation.

Formulated in response to multiple sessions of dialogue with museum staff, neighborhood residents, and external constituencies, the MCA's charge to Garofalo Architects was to be "architecturally and programmatically innovative in the ways that design, audience, and dialogue, merge, intersect, and inform each other." The commission was intended to stimulate new educational and outreach programs and bond the process of designing and building to the conceptual and critical process associated with architectural practice. Such an elastic responsibility might seem disproportional, even burdensome, for a project that lasted for only six months, but

88

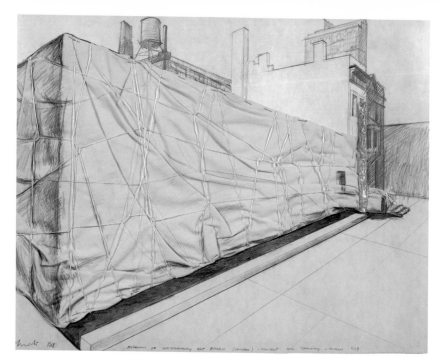

the commission privileged egalitarian activity over more conventional architectural criteria and elegant photographic mementos. In conjunction with this project and UIC's College of Architecture and the Arts, Garofalo also conducted a graduate seminar in which art historians, architects, and artists explored the history of public art in relation to the design and building process.

Explicitly emphasizing the architectural significance of "between" as a theoretical premise, Garofalo Architects has a history of positioning its work on the edges of theory and practice, objects and space. Its designs often project an intention to bridge disciplinary boundaries — for example, to intersect real and ideal design. Moreover, Garofalo Architects search out and experiment with new materials for traditional and untraditional construction. And while on one hand, the MCA project fits into a tradition of site-specific artwork, the firm has also had substantial success considering museum audiences for the Museum of Science and Industry, The Art Institute of Chicago, and the Smart Museum, among others. Garofalo Architects' propensity for dialectical engagement, its concentration on the interstices of design and construction, has also been foregrounded by the impact of digital media in design, whether in the Korean Presbyterian Church in Queens or most recently for the Hyde Park Art Center's permanent home.

In downtown Chicago the tradition of public sculpture is embodied in major works by Pablo Picasso, Alexander Calder, and Claes Oldenburg and continually reinvigorated through an active percent-for-art program that commissions site-specific works. Indeed, the centerpiece of Millennium Park, itself a collection of prestigious architectural commissions designed to become a cultural destination for visitors, will be a major sculpture by London-based artist Anish Kapoor. Chicago planners capitalized on the expectation that experimental art should be allowed to transgress the conventional when the Frank Gehry Music Pavilion, despite its failure to conform to building-code standards, was granted an exemption when reclassified as sculpture, rather than architecture. To the south of the city, twenty-two large-scale outdoor sculptures are permanently installed on the 750-acre campus of Governors State University in the Nathan Manilow Sculpture Park. From 1983 to 1996, the opportunities for real-estate development and art came together under the auspices of *Sculpture Chicago*, spearheaded by U.S. Equities Realty chairman Robert A. Wislow. This organization commissioned dozens of works by an international group of artists including Richard Deacon, Vito Acconci, Dan Peterman, and Judith Shea. *Culture in Action* (1995), the most challenging iteration of this series, orchestrated unconventional partnerships of artists and community groups that teamed together to produce temporary events and alternatives to museum exhibitions. Artists such as Mark Dion, Iñigo Manglano-Ovalle with Street Level Video, and the Chicago collaborative Haha — Richard House, Wendy Jacob, Laurie Palmer, and John Ploof — all worked in specific Chicago neighborhoods. Haha developed a storefront hydroponic garden called *Flood: A Volunteer Network for Active Partcipation in Healthcare*, which produced food and educational programs for persons with HIV, stressing the potential of survival as a metaphor for caregiving and sharing. Mark Dion's practice employed the museum exhibition model as the stimulus for his work with the public, working first with high school sculpture students in environmental study groups to build displays for a wildlife sanctuary in Belize. *Sculpture Chicago*'s emphasis on process enabled these artists to engage multiple constituencies in the creation process and weave their artwork into the everyday lives of their audiences.

89

Gordon Matta-Clark
Installation detail of
Circus or The Caribbean Orange, 1978
© 2003 Estate of
Gordon Matta-Clark /
Artists Rights Society
(ARS), New York

Between Art and Architecture

Numerous artists and architects have intentionally ignored the lines between disciplines to remarkable effect. Los Angeles sculptor Jorge Pardo, for instance, constructed and opened his home to visitors as a hybrid art installation; the firm Lot/Ek creates mobile dwelling units. Between 1995 and 2002, Vienna's MAK Center for Art and Architecture convened eight artists and architects working together in Los Angeles. But perhaps the most influential theoretician of the architecture of the imaginary is John Hejduk, whose revered status derives from his drawings and poetry rather than conventional buildings. Also on this spectrum of exchange between the architectonic and the aesthetic is the practice of Diller + Scofidio, which also depends on a combination of electronic media, performance, and design and is best known for their conceptual proposals. The gorgeous impermanence of Diller + Scofidio's Blur Building in Switzerland (2002, p. 87) presented a most dramatic example of architectural dematerialization. Visitors walked across a ramp on Lake Neuchâtel to reach the elevated platform; the pavilion covered by an enormous, man-made, constantly changing cloud of fog generated by 30,000 tiny sprays. Other crossovers between architecture and artistic practice can be seen in Chicago in the architectural projects of Vito Acconci, one of the most important figures of conceptual and minimal art, whose work now is exclusively architectural. Adjacent to the central administrative building of the University of Illinois at Chicago, Acconci Studio has designed a block-long plaza crisscrossed by diagonal pathways and shallow pools. Loosely related to the grid of the twenty-eight-story building, the new plaza plan calls for awnings attached to the building entries woven from steel cable and covered by vines. Twenty-eight miles southwest of Chicago, Dan Graham's *Pavilion/Sculpture for Argonne* (1981) was inspired by the park pavilions of European royalty and Reitveld's pavilion in the sculpture park of the Kroller-Muller museum. Influenced by the glass home Mies van der Rohe designed for Dr. Edith Farnsworth in nearby Plano and on the occasion of an administrative complex designed by Helmut Jahn, Graham produced a fifteen-by-fifteen-foot structure that exists as shelter, with interior and exterior space, yet deliberately celebrates its dual character as both architecture and sculpture. Using mirror and glass, spectators view themselves,

Beat Streuli
Chicago, July 99, (detail), 1999
Silver dye-bleach transparencies on Plexiglas
Overall dimensions variable, each of sixty-eight parts: 63 × 63 in. (160 × 160 cm)
Collection Museum of Contemporary Art, Chicago, restricted gift of the Collectors Forum; support for original commission from Sara Albrecht and Bill Nygren

OPPOSITE
Dan Peterman
Accessories to an Event (plaza) (detail), 1998
Reprocessed plastic
Dimensions variable
Collection Museum of Contemporary Art, Chicago, restricted gift of Sara Albrecht and Bill Nygren

Redmoon Theater
Galway's Shadow, 2001

OPPOSITE
Tobias Rehberger
*The Sun from Above
(Die Sonne von oben)*
(detail), 2000
Museum of
Contemporary Art,
Chicago, commission
with support by Sara
Albrecht and Bill Nygren;
Diane and Robert M.
Levy; and Michael La
Porta and Rick Easty of
Bell Construction, Inc.

Between the Museum and the City

viewing the sculpture, viewing the park.
In construction on the corner of Halsted and
Roosevelt Road, a major new sky space by
James Turrell will invite city dwellers inside.
In this softly lit oval structure, thirty-two feet
in diameter and open to the sky, viewers
will contemplate myriad changes in light and
unexpected perceptual awareness.

Between the Museum and the City also
belongs to a context of architectural innova-
tions associated with museums. In New
York, P.S.1/MOMA has developed a compe-
tition to invite public projects for their
Young Architects Series. In London, the
Serpentine Gallery annually commissions
international architects of worldwide acclaim
to "design a pavilion for the gallery's lawn
that provides a unique showcase for contemporary architectural practice." From its
earliest history in a more modest building
on Ontario Street, the MCA has created its
own tradition of using its building as material and backdrop for artistic interventions.
In 1969, Christo and his partner Jeanne-
Claude wrapped the exterior and draped the
lower galleries in 8,000 square feet of cotton
drop cloth (see p. 88); their work denied the
very function of the institution while trans-
forming it into a work of art. Less than a

decade later, Gordon Matta-Clark created his last major public project, *Circus or The Caribbean Orange*, by slicing open the museum annex for a temporary exhibition that would become enormously significant for artists and architects (see p. 89). Other projects that brought the two disciplines together in dialogue include facade alterations by Michael Asher, benches and ramps made from recycled plastic on the plaza by Dan Peterman (p. 90), and a "garden sculpture" by Tobias Rehberger, as well as numerous works created for the facade of the current building by artists such as Beat Streuli and Julian Opie. Redmoon Theater's *Galway's Shadow* (2001) transformed the building's front windows into a giant shadow-puppet theater.

As the Garofalo installation formally wove social space into specific seasonal and educational activities, it integrated community participation, inventive city planning, and experimental public sculpture. Although the architects located the project conceptually and spatially "between" the museum and the city, their notion of weaving provided a conceptual linkage when the armature climbed down the stairs and into the park. Celebrating its provisional nature as conse-

quential, *Between the Museum and the City* galvanized the principle of accessibility and its own interactive agenda. Taking advantage of the flexibility allowed to artistic imagination, the project realized the shifting distinctions between institutional and architectural stability. It punctuated the dynamics of the relationship between a museum's mission of public access, its transparency, and its

responsibility to collection and containment. At night, populated by young people and illuminated by tiny LED lights, *Between the Museum and the City* became a hybrid landscape, revisualizing the museum's boundaries as a migrating zone of place relations open to varied audiences and unlimited meanings.

1 See James Meyer, "The Functional Site," *Documents*, no. 7, pp. 20–29.

2 Ibid.

93

ABOUT GAROFALO ARCHITECTS, INC.

Garofalo Architects is an award-winning, internationally recognized practice located in Chicago that attempts to produce critical work through buildings, projects, research, and teaching. All members within the firm engage both professional and academic realms as a means to relate the practical with the theoretical, actively seeking out collective and interdisciplinary teams for the purposes of producing innovative buildings. For more than ten years Garofalo Architects has produced critically acclaimed buildings, offices, exhibition designs, installations, and commercial spaces.

Members of Garofalo Architects participating in *Between the Museum and the City*

Julie Flohr, Project Manager

Randall Kober

Carl Karlen

Douglas Garofalo

Christine Garofalo

Garofalo Architects, Inc., would like to acknowledge the generous efforts and assistance with on-site construction and fabrication of the following students from the graduate elective class at the School of Architecture, University of Illinois at Chicago:

Will Corcoran

Nicole Covarribias

Kenneth Glazer

Colin Morgan

Siamak Mostoufi

Masha Safina

Karla Sierralta

Brian Strawn

Bill Turoczy

SELECTED PROJECTS

Current work

APPS • PITTSBURGH, installation at the Carnegie Museum of Art, Pittsburgh

Hyde Park Art Center, Chicago

Millennium Park Terraces, with Xavier Vendrell Studio, Chicago

Nothstine Residence, Green Bay, Wis.

Punmit Residence, Ban Mae Sot, Thailand

Completed work

Baisi Thai Restaurant, Oakbrook, Ill.

Boston Pier Restaurant, Beijing

Chen Residence, Winnetka, Ill.

Chowaniec Residence, Glenview, Ill.

Dawoud Bey: The Chicago Project in Collaboration with Dan Collison and Elizabeth Meister, The David and Alfred Smart Museum of Art, The University of Chicago

Derman Residence, Skokie, Ill.

94

Dub Residence, Highland Park, Ill.

Earth From Above, with Digit-All Studio, Chicago

Faces, Places, and Inner Spaces, The Art Institute of Chicago

Gary Residence, Ada, Mich.

The Hub Lobby Design, Chicago

In.Formant System prototype, Museum of Contemporary Art, Chicago, and Yale University, New Haven, Conn.

Kipnis Residence, Chicago

Malter Residence, Chicago

Manilow Residence, Spring Prairie, Wis.

Markow Residence, Prospect Heights, Ill.

New York Presbyterian Church, with Lynn Form and Michael McInturf Architects, New York

Offices of Thornton Tomasetti Engineers, Chicago

OYSY Restaurant, Chicago

Pacific Rim Kitchen, Northbrook, Ill.

Randolph Station Lofts, Chicago

Strauss Residence, Winnetka, Ill.

Time, Museum of Science and Industry, Chicago

28 Shop, Marshall Field's, Chicago

2001: Design for Space Travel, The Art Institute of Chicago

Typhoon Restaurant, Chicago

Visual Effects Optical, Chicago

Numerous individuals provided critical support and feedback. Garofalo Architects wishes specifically to acknowledge the efforts of Greg Cameron at the MCA and Jane Saks at UIC. Stephen Hokanson, Senior Preparator at the MCA, demonstrated not only great skill and craft, but generous patience with us as a fabrication team.

All photographs provided by the Museum of Contemporary Art, Chicago, and Garofalo Architects, Inc., unless otherwise indicated.

95

Garofalo Architects